Creative Fabric
Decoration

Published in 1995 by Grange Books
An imprint of Grange Books PLC
The Grange
Grange Yard
London SE1 3AG

ISBN 1 85627 771 2

Printed in China.

The Author and Publishers would like to thank the
following people who kindly donated their goods.

MARBLING KIT

Philip and Tacey Ltd
North Way
Andover
SP10 5BA

BOW TIES

Cut Outs
87 Church Road
Hanwell
London
W7 3BH

DYES AND FIXATIVE

Dylon International Ltd
Worsley Bridge Road
Lower Sydenham
London
SE26 5HD

RIBBONS AND ROSEBUDS

CM Offray and Sons Ltd
Suppliers of Ribbons
Fir Tree Place
Church Road
Ashford
Middlesex
TW15 2PH

DIAMANTÉ AND METAL TRIMS

Creative Bead Craft
(Mail Order)
Unit 26 Chiltern Trading Estate
Earl Howe Road
Holmer Green
High Wycombe
Buckinghamshire

Creative Fabric
Decoration

Letty Oates

Grange
BOOKS

CONTENTS

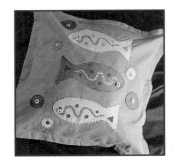

INTRODUCTION

Creative Fabric Decoration encompasses a multitude of crafts and items to make and decorate. In this book, with the help of clear step-by-step photographs and illustrations, the work of a variety of artists is demonstrated. They have let us into their secrets to show us how to make and decorate many items including clothes, hats, lingerie and waistcoats for children and adults.

There are accessories for the home such as cushion covers, table mats, a table cloth and even a mirror. Children have not been left out: there is a pencil case, a striking painted mat for a child's room and painting smocks. The techniques covered range from the simplest marbling project through to a modern and quick method of tie-dye to the more complex appliqué techniques as demonstrated in the work of Sarah King.

Most of the projects can easily be done in an evening. Few need specialist equipment and many use inexpensive materials. There are 32 projects in the book which I know you will agree will give you more than enough food for thought.

LETTY OATES

The lace we have used for this cushion is in fact new. It has been dyed using tea to give it an antique look. Exquisite narrow blue ribbon has been chosen for the finishing touch.

WHERE TO FIND OLD LACE

Look out for odd pieces of lace in antique, thrift, or charity shops; go to jumble sales and auctions. The big auction houses hold special textile sales where you can often pick up a case of lace.

An old dress or a tray cloth with a lace edging can often be unpicked. Old lace hankies and antimacassars can all be turned into cushion covers. Don't reject a piece of lace because it has rust marks. These can always be covered up or disguised in some way or other. A piece of lace that has been a cuff or collar may already be slightly gathered. If this is the case, use it as a frill.

THE CARE OF LACE

Old lace should be kept in a dry, warm atmosphere and if it is stored for any length of time it should be taken out and aired at frequent intervals to prevent mould forming. Often, old lace consists of a heavy pattern set on a net background. Usually it is the background which wears thin or rips first. Use the non-worn part of the lace as a motif or sewn onto replacement net.

MATERIALS

Enough lace to cover the front of the cushion

2¹⁄₂ times the cushion's circumference in wide and narrow lace and 1m extra of wide lace to make a bow

Piece of blue satin to make the cushion front and back

Heart-shaped cushion pad, pale blue and white thread and a needle

Sewing machine, scissors

Tea or tea bag and a bowl

HOW TO AGE LACE

Prepare a very strong pot of tea, pour this into a bowl and leave the lace to soak in it. The longer you leave the lace the darker the shade will be. For a subtly different shade, try soaking the lace in coffee.

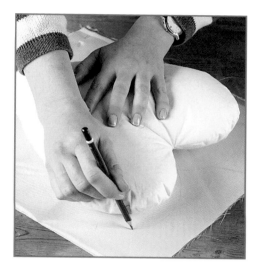

1 Fold the piece of satin so that there are two layers. Place cushion pad on the satin and draw round it. Cut the heart shape out leaving 1cm (¼ in) seam allowance. With right sides together sew along seam allowance leaving a gap large enough to insert cushion pad. Snip round the edges before turning cover right side out. Press.

3 Sew enough wide strips of lace together. Use these to cover the front of the cushion following its shape and sewing them neatly into place.

5 Cut lengths of narrow blue ribbon and sew in double rows over the lace joins in the cushion front, catching it in at the edges of the cushion. Make blue ribbon bows and sew into the ends of the double rows.

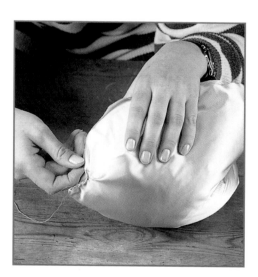

2 Insert pad into cushion cover and close the opening by oversewing neatly.

4 To make the frill, cut a broad and narrow piece of lace two-and-a-half times the perimeter of the cushion pad. This will make a full frill. Place the narrow lace on top of the wide lace. Using a large running stitch, sew through the two thicknesses of lace along one long edge. Draw up the running stitches and pin and then sew it all around the cushion.

6 Finish off the cushion by making a large lace bow and attach it at several points using invisible stitches.

Pretty satin ballet shoes are ideal for transforming into party or fancy dress shoes. They can then be dyed or embellished with lace, sequins and diamanté. For this step-by-step sequence we used lace doilies and tiny pearl buttons.

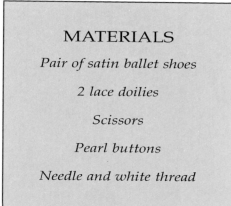

MATERIALS

Pair of satin ballet shoes

2 lace doilies

Scissors

Pearl buttons

Needle and white thread

1 Cut the centre motif out of one of the doilies and use it to decorate the front of the shoe, using the remainder on the sides.

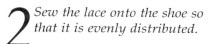

2 Sew the lace onto the shoe so that it is evenly distributed.

3 Sew the border of the doily in a band round the top of the shoe.

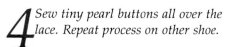

4 Sew tiny pearl buttons all over the lace. Repeat process on other shoe.

This attractive hat will add a fashionable look to any winter outfit. Though relatively simple to make, a very professional look can easily be achieved.

Our hat has been decorated with plastic bobbles, but you can use glass or ceramic beads or pretty buttons.

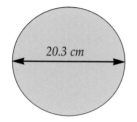

20.3 cm

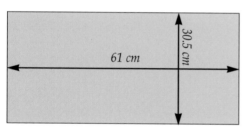

61 cm

30.5 cm

1 To make the pattern for the crown draw a 20.3cm (8ins) diameter circle onto paper. Cut out. Pin the pattern onto black wool and cut out. Repeat with the red lining fabric. Using the white pencil and ruler, draw a large rectangle measuring 61cm x 30.5cm (24ins x 12ins) on the remaining black wool fabric. Cut out. With right sides together, fold the rectangle in half so that the short edges meet.

2 Sew the two ends together to make a wide hat-band. Press the seam open. Fold the band in half with the wrong sides inside, stitch together 5mm (1/8in) from the edge.

3 Pin and sew the stitched edge of the band to the crown.

4 With right sides together, sandwich the hat-band between the woollen crown and the red lining. Pin and sew around the circle edge, 1cm (¼ in) in from the edge. Leave a 9cm (3½ ins) opening somewhere in between the beginning and the end of stitching. Pull the hat through the opening and sew up the gap.

5 Sew the beads along the bottom of the hat-band and fold the edge up towards the top to form a cuff.

This waistcoat was ready-made. However, it is much easier to attach appliqué to pieces of fabric at the cut-out stage, before the garment has been full assembled. It is possible to decorate an existing waistcoat but this is rather more difficult for a beginner to tackle.

So before you start, buy a pattern and cut out the waistcoat. The fabric in the illustration is a heavy raw silk. Templates for the ivy pattern are in the back of the book.

MATERIALS

Purchased paper pattern for a waistcoat

Fabric according to the pattern

Dressmakers' scissors

Fabric for making appliqué

Use of a photocopier

Tracing paper

Double-sided fusible webbing

Embroidery scissors, iron, sewing-machine and thread

1 Using the templates, copy the ivy design onto tracing paper or enlarge it first on a photocopier if you wish it to be larger in scale.

3 Using very sharp embroidery scissors, cut out the shapes to be appliquéd.

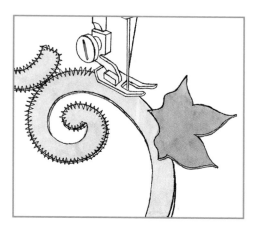

5 Using a zig zag stitch sew round the edge of each shape. Make up the rest of the waistcoat according to the instructions in the pattern.

2 Trace the design onto the backing paper of the fusible webbing and iron it onto the back of the coloured fabrics which will make up the appliquéd design.

4 Peel away the backing paper and then pin the shapes on the waistcoat fronts. Iron the shapes into position, following the manufacturers instructions for the correct heat setting and timing.

This is an elegant way to make storage boxes for shoes, jewellery, photographs or other precious items. Cover the box in one solid colour or you could use a combination of contrasting shades. Enhance your design with lace or appliqué to make a complementary accessory for any room.

MATERIALS

Shoe box and wadding to fit lid.

Copydex or fabric glue, paper for cutting pattern

Fabric to cover the box, ruler and pencil, scissors

NOTE: Use non-fray fabrics or treat them with roller blind spray.

1 Using the lid of the box as a guide, cut out paper pattern as shown in the picture. Cut wadding to fit the lid and stick to the top. Using the pattern, cut the fabric for the lid and stick this onto the lid over the wadding as shown.

2 Measure the inside of the lid and cut a piece of backing fabric. Stick this onto the inside of the lid.

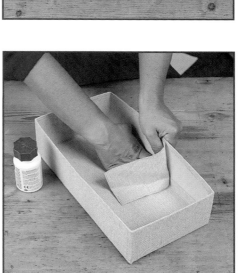

3 Measure both the inside and the outside of the box and cut a strip of fabric slightly larger in dimension to allow for overlap. Stick fabric to the outside of the box snipping the corners.

4 Repeat step three for the inside of the box. Stick fabric on the base of the box to finish.

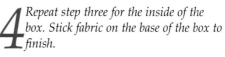

These decorative all-purpose aprons are so useful that they can double up as bibs, overalls or painting smocks. Just choose your theme and get to work. They are made from wipe-down PVC and decorated with sticky-backed plasticized material (Fablon). This material comes in plain colours, transparent, and a variety of patterns.

1 Using the template, scale up the main pattern to fit your child. Pin the pattern on the PVC material and cut out twice. With right sides together, join the shoulder seams. Turn under all raw edges and sew with a running stitch. Cut the tape into four equal lengths. Measure up 21cm (8½ins) from the bottom edge of the smock. Sew a tape to each side edge at this point to make the ties. Trace required decorative patterns onto paper and cut out the traced shapes.

2 With a ball-point pen, draw round the templates transferring them to the back of the sticky-backed plastic.

4 Tear off the backing paper from the background shapes and stick them onto the apron.

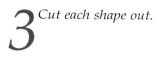

3 Cut each shape out.

These beautiful curtains, made from lightweight muslin and decorated with fabric paints are a welcome addition to any room. Design your own stencils to match your wallpaper and furnishings.

1 Cut the curtains and loops to the required length. Most curtains take 2½ to 3 times the width of the window. The loops are designed for a window pole. Press the fabric flat. Trace the design from the back of the book onto stencil card. Place the stencil card on the mat and cut out the design.

2 Put lots of paper on the work table to protect it as muslin is a very thin fabric. Alternatively, place an old sheet under it. Tape the muslin down to prevent it moving around. Tape a band of masking tape to mark where the first colour finishes and dab the colour through the stencil.

3 When dry, apply the second colour beneath the masking tape band. Leave to dry. When dry, iron the fabric on the back to fix the colour.

4 Neaten the edge of the curtains and make the loops. Sew the loops so that they are evenly spaced along the top edge of the curtain.

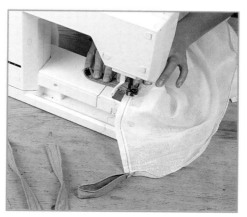

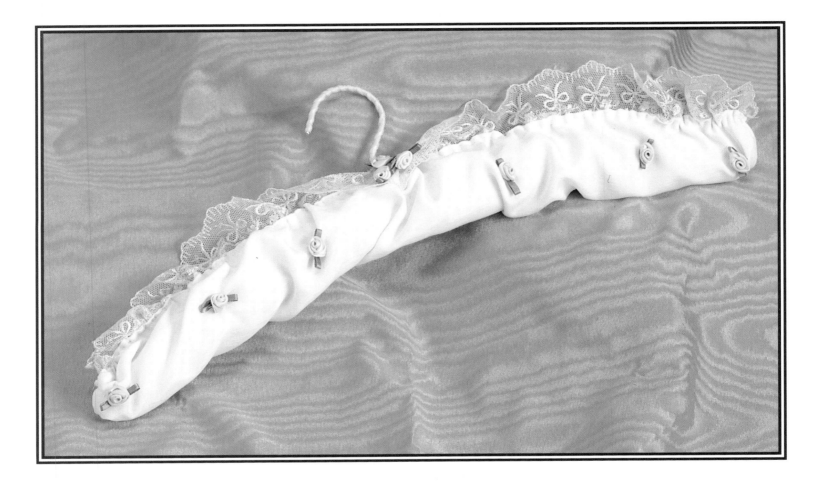

Padded coat-hangers are very easy to make and are a must for protecting expensive or delicate clothes. Adapt your choice of fabric for a more masculine version.

MATERIALS

140cm x 10cm (55ins x 4ins) wadding or a strip double the length of the coat-hanger.

60cm x 15cm (24ins x 6ins) strip of material

60cm (24ins) length of lace

Wooden coat-hanger

Needle and thread

1.5m (56ins) narrow ribbon

Craft glue

Packet of ribbon rosebuds

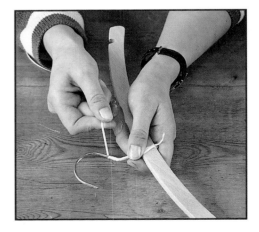

1 Wind the narrow ribbon round the metal hook of the coat-hanger until it is completely covered. Dab some glue on the end of the ribbon and hold it in place until dry.

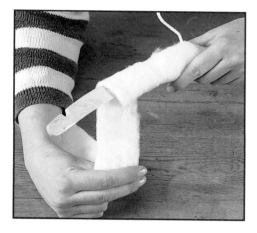

2 Wind the wadding round the coat hanger so that it is even, dab the ends with some glue and hold until dry.

3 Fold the fabric in half and place a pin to mark the centre. Draw a curve to follow the sides of the coat-hanger and cut out the curve.

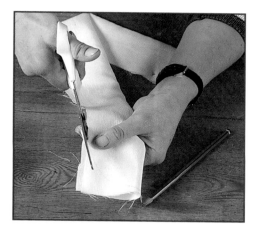

4 Turn under the edges to make a seam allowance of 6mm ($^1/_8$ in) and iron into place.

5 Tapering the sides, sew the length of lace along one edge of the fabric.

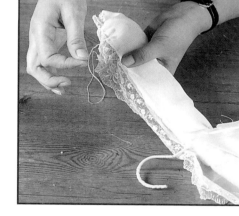

6 Mark the centre of the fabric with the lace at the top. Fold the fabric round the hanger and sew the sides together, gathering as you go, working from one side to the centre and then from the other side to the centre.

7 Catch the centre of the lace by the hook and sew a few stitches. Decorate by sewing on rosebud bows.

ELEPHANT CUSHION

This attractive cushion will appeal to both children and adults alike. It is relatively simple to make. Adapt the design to make other favourite animals. It works just as well as a cuddly toy.

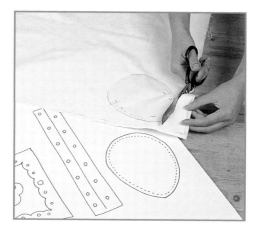

1 Trace the elephant, ear, saddle and saddle strap shapes from the back of the book. Enlarge the shapes to the size you wish the finished cushion to be by using the enlarging section of a photocopier. Pin the elephant shape onto two layers of plain calico. Pin two ear shapes to the double thickness of calico. (You will then have four ear shapes). Pin the saddle and strap to one layer of calico. Cut them all out.

3 Take the two large elephant pieces and pin with the right sides together, placing a piece of wool for the tail in the seam on the back. With right sides facing, make the ears into pairs and sew round the edge. Sew the body and the ears leaving a gap for filling with stuffing. Snip into the curved edges.

4 Fill the ears with a little stuffing and the elephant body with a large amount. To make the saddle turn the edges under to neaten and sew with a running stitch. Sew the strap to one side of the saddle.

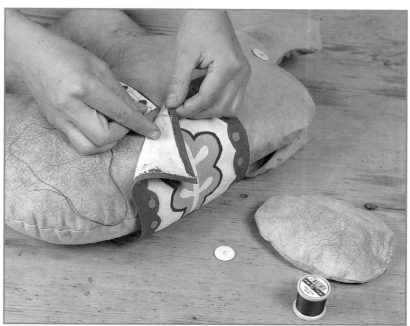

2 Place all the calico pieces onto a piece of paper on top of the work surface. Either sponge or apply the colour onto the main body shape using a large brush. Allow to dry and then iron on the wrong side to fix. Using the pattern as a guide, paint the saddle and strap in other colours with fabric felt pens. Press all the pieces of fabric.

5 Close the gap in the elephant body and the gap in the ears. Sew the ears onto the body. Add a button to either side of the head for the eyes. Place the saddle on the elephant's back and stitch the strap to the other side to secure it.

23

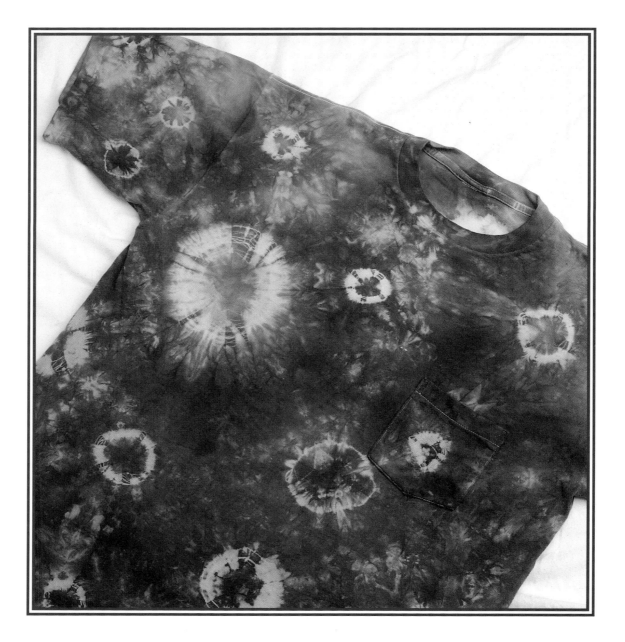

Tie-dye is one of the oldest methods of fabric decoration, and has always been very popular. Here we show you a very fast and modern way of doing it, using a microwave oven.

MATERIALS

*Microwave oven, non metallic bowl, clingfilm (saran wrap), spoon,
hand or machine dye, salt, fixative
Rubber gloves, tee shirt to dye, thread, pebbles or gravel, iron*

1 Decide on the kind of pattern you want and bind or tie the cloth accordingly. The tighter the binding the stronger the resist. Circles are made by placing pebbles in the tee shirt and binding with cotton.

2 Put on rubber gloves. Mix dye with fixative, salt and water in the non-metallic bowl. Stir so there are no lumps. (Quantities will depend on the dye system being used).

3 Soak the tee shirt in water before it goes into the dye bath to ensure a sharp and even colour on the unbound areas. Squeeze out the excess moisture. Put the tee shirt in the bowl of dye and agitate it so that it will dye evenly. If necessary, add more water to cover the tee shirt.

4 Cover the bowl loosely with clingfilm to allow steam to escape. Place the bowl in microwave oven for 2 minutes on full power. Remove and lift clingfilm. Stir mixture and tee shirt. Put back the clingfilm and microwave for a further 2 minutes.

5 Remove the bowl from the microwave oven and rinse the tee shirt under running water. Leave it to dry and then, using an unpicker, carefully undo all the ties.

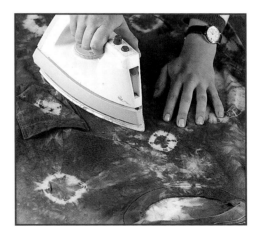

6 When all the ties have been undone, iron the fabric to reveal the pattern.

The French beret will always be classic headwear. Here we make two berets out of black wool and decorate them with coloured embroidery and raffia patterns. This will add a brilliant splash of colour to these stylish hats.

TAPESTRY BERET

MATERIALS

For each beret, black wool measuring 100cm x 28cm (39ins x 11½ins)

Pins, ruler, pencil, white pencil

Compass and pattern paper, scissors, tapestry needle, needle and black sewing thread

FOR TAPESTRY BERET
1 x skein of each of the following colours of tapestry wools: orange, dark green, light green, yellow, pink, light blue, dark blue, brown, rust

FOR RAFFIA BERET
Artificial raffia in various colours cut into 4m lengths
1 x large crochet hook (5.50mm)

3 With wrong sides facing, fold the smaller rectangle in half. Pin short edges together and stitch 1 cm (1/4in) in from the edge to form a ring. Press the seam open. Fold the ring with wrong sides together in half and stay stitch the raw edges together to form the headband.

1 Using the compass and pencil make a circle of 21.5cm (8½ins) diameter onto paper to make the crown pattern. Cut out. Pin the pattern onto black wool and cut out. Using the white pencil and ruler, draw 2 large rectangles, one measuring 67cm x 10cm (26½ins x 4ins), the other 62cm x 7cm (25in x 3ins) on the remaining black wool fabric. Cut them out. Following the illustration, mark the stalk positions on the right side of the fabric using a white pencil or tailor's chalk. Embroider the flowers around the stalks using the different coloured wools. Use a variety of stitches including back- and stem-stitch for the stalks and daisy-, satin-stitch and couching for the flowers.

2 Take the longer rectangle of fabric and fold it in half with wrong sides facing. Pin short edges together and stitch 1cm (1/4in) in from the edge to form a ring. Press the seam open. On the right side of this 'hat ring' embroider 2 wavy lines of back-stitch (one brown and one rust). Embroider yellow and red flowers at random along the wavy lines. Finish with dark and light green satin-stitched leaves.

4 Make up the hat by pinning with right sides facing the embroidered crown to the hat ring. Stitch in place 1cm (1/4in) in from the edges. With right sides together, pin embroidered headband to embroidered hat ring. Stitch in place 1cm (1/4in) from the edge. Sew the raw edges with tapestry wool to neaten them. Turn finished hat right side out.

1 Using the compass and pencil, make a circle of 21.5cm (8½ins) diameter onto paper to make the crown pattern. Cut out. Pin the pattern onto black wool and cut out. Using the white pencil and ruler, draw 2 large rectangles one measuring 67cm x 10cm (26½ins x 4ins), the other 62cm x 7cm (25ins x 3ins) on the remaining black wool fabric. Cut them out. Take the longer rectangle of fabric and fold it in half with wrong sides facing. Pin short edges together and stitch 1cm (1/4in) in from the edge to form a ring. Press the seam open. With wrong sides facing, fold the smaller rectangle in half. Fold the ring with wrong sides together in half and stay-stitch the raw edges together to form the headband.

2 Make up the hat by pinning, with right sides facing, the crown to the hat ring. Stitch in place 1cm (¼in) in from the edges. With right sides together, pin headband to the hat ring and stitch in place 1cm (¼in) from the edge. Sew the raw edges with tapestry wool to neaten them.

28

3 TO MAKE LONG RAFFIA CHAINS
Take 2 strands of raffia and, using a
5.50mm hook, crotchet 25-35 chains.
Make 6-8 lengths of raffia in different colours.
Cast off. Cut raffia ends approx. 40cm (16ins)
from the last chain.
TO MAKE RINGS
Crotchet 4-5 rings of raffia in different colours
as follows: Take 2 strands of raffia and, using
a 5.50mm hook, crotchet 5 chains to form a
ring. Make 1 chain, 10 double crotchet into
ring. Slip stitch in first double crochet. Cast
off. Cut raffia approx. 20cm (8ins) from last
stitch.

4 Arrange raffia chains and rings over and
around the beret. Pin them into position.
Using the long ends of raffia, stitch the
shapes in place, with a tapestry needle.

Note: Raffia shapes can be plaited instead of
crocheted, and thick, brightly-coloured wools
may be used as an alternative to raffia.

As a change from plain, tablecloths can be transformed by this simple method of fabric decoration. You can use the same method to make matching table napkins.

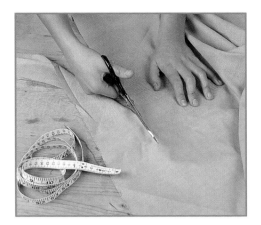

1 Measure out the piece of cloth and cut to the required size. Press flat. Choose paper doilies with a pleasing design. The larger the holes the better.

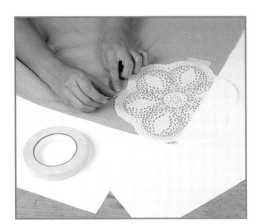

2 Place paper on the work surface and lay the cloth on top. Place the chosen doily onto the edge of the cloth and hold it down with masking tape.

3 Stencil the colour through the doily moving the brush in an up-and-down motion to stamp the colour through it. Leave the design to dry and press with a hot iron on the back to fix. Proceed in the same way until the required design has been achieved all along the cloth.

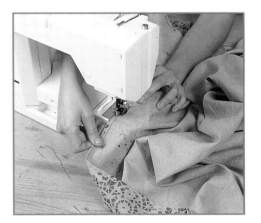

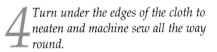

4 Turn under the edges of the cloth to neaten and machine sew all the way round.

MATERIALS

Piece of linen/cotton fabric big enough to make a cloth for your table. (You can buy sheeting for this purpose)

Paper doilies, sewing machine, fabric paints, iron, scissors, pins

Masking tape, stencil brush

This brightly-coloured floor mat is hard-wearing, will add a splash of colour to a child's room and makes an ideal play accessory.

MATERIALS

Fabric pencil

Approximately 1m (39ins) of canvas or thick calico

Acrylic paints

Paint brushes in a variety of sizes

Matt acrylic varnish

Strong needle and thread

Carbon paper

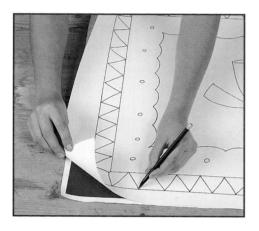

1 Cut out one piece of canvas 50cm x 90cm (20ins x 36ins). Cut another piece 1cm larger all the way round than the other. Trace the horse using the template from the back of the book and enlarge it on a photocopier. Place a piece of carbon paper under the template and on top of the canvas. Trace over the design to transfer it to the canvas below.

2 Using various coloured acrylic paints and different sized brushes, paint the design onto the canvas. Use large brushes for large areas and small brushes for details. Leave to dry. Apply three or four layers of clear acrylic varnish, allowing it to dry between coats.

4 Paint with a coat of clear acrylic matt varnish.

3 Sew the top mat to the bottom one, turning under the edges of the larger onto the one underneath to neaten. Use a large needle and simple stitches along the edge of the mat for a decorative finish.

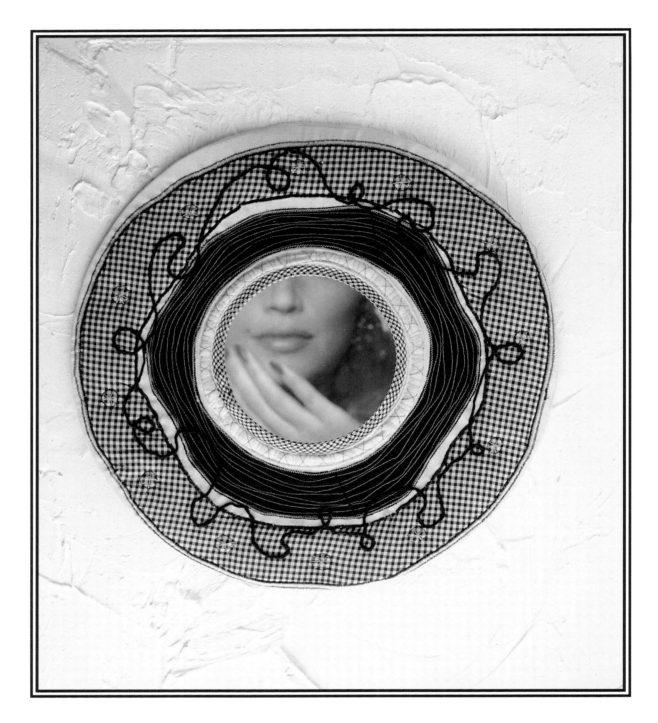

Mirrors can look different and exciting when framed in appliquéd fabric. This strong black-and-white motif is attractive and would brighten up any room in the house. Vary the colours to give a lively effect to each room.

1 In the centre of the calico cut a circle with a 20cm (8ins) diameter. Neaten edge by sewing on black-and-white bias binding.

MATERIALS

Mirror tile

50cm (20ins) calico

Circle of card with a diameter of 46cm (18½ins)

2m (2½yds) 2cm wide bias binding in a natural colour

1m (1¼yds) black-and-white bias binding

50cm (20ins) black-and-white gingham

32cm (12¾ins) black cotton fabric

Black and white sewing thread

Black cord, pins, scissors sewing-machine, string

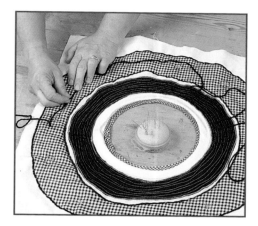

4 Sew a rope pattern over the gingham and black portions of the mirror frame. Finish off white inner ring with a decorative cross-stitch. (See main picture).

2 Cut a bias strip of calico 5cm (2ins) wide and to the perimeter of the circle. Turn in the outer edges, fold in half and pin in position round the outside edge of the black-and-white bias binding to form a thick border. Sew into position.

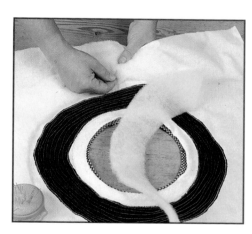

5 Trim away excess fabric leaving 3cm (1½ins) border all round to be turned under. Place the mirror tile in position and cover the back with strong glue. Place the cardboard over the mirror tile. Attach the calico to the card with string threaded from one side of the mirror crossing to the other.

3 Cut a 5cm (2ins) wide ring of black fabric with an inside diameter of 22cm (8¾ins). Place this on the calico and sew into position with a zig-zag edge and lines of decorative white stitching in the centre. Cut a wadding ring with a 37cm (14¾ins) diameter, the ring itself being 5cm (2ins) wide. Pin onto the wadding and cover with the gingham fabric.

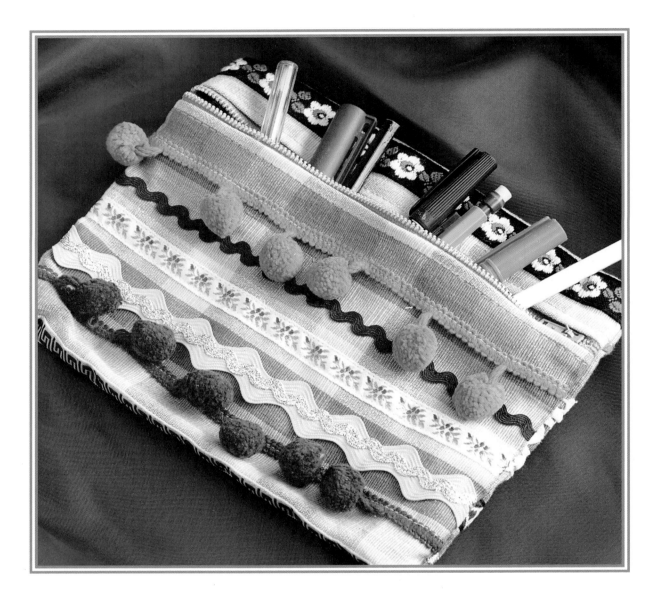

Make yourself a very individual pencil case, or even some for the children. Choose bright fabric and fun ric-rac and other braids to make a striking design which could be varied with pretty fabric and lace to create a vanity bag.

MATERIALS

36cm x 25cm (14ins x 10ins) rectangle of heavy-weight cotton fabric

A selection of ribbons, lace, pom-pom braid and ric-rac (each measuring 25cm (10ins)

1 x 9ins zip, needle, pins, sewing thread, scissors, ruler

1 *Place the rectangle of fabric right side up on the work surface with the 36cm (14ins) edges running lengthways. Arrange the braids across the width in rows. Pin into position.*

2 *Add more and more braids and finish about 2-3cm from the bottom of the cloth. Sew into position.*

3 *Centre the zip with its right side facing the right side of the fabric. Pin and stitch zip close to teeth along the top edge of the fabric. Flip the zip over so that the right side faces up and top-stitch the seam flat. Repeat step 3 with the zip and the lower edge of the fabric.*

4 *Close the zip three-quarters of the way along. Turn bag so right sides are on inside. Crease the top and bottom edges so zip lies 3.5cm (1½ins) down from the top crease and approximately 13cm (5ins) up from the bottom. Pin the side seams together and stitch 1cm in from the edges. Neaten the seams with a zig-zag or blanket-stitch.*

5 *Open zip fully and turn the bag right side out.*

MATERIALS

Lining fabric

Wadding or kapok

Pieces of fabric to make patchwork

Needle and thread

Sewing-machine

These pin-cushions are too pretty to be hidden away in a drawer or work-basket. To make the roses for the hat-pin cushion you can use the same method as that shown on page 44. For this project, we are going to make the patchwork pin-cushion at the top of the picture.

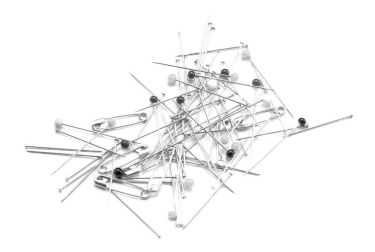

1 *Cut two squares of lining fabric 10cm x 10cm (4ins x 4ins) and one piece of lining fabric 42cm x 12cm (16¾ ins x 4¾ ins). With wrong sides together, sew the wide piece of fabric onto the first square and then sew the two 12cm seams of the long piece of fabric together. Sew the other square onto the opening around three sides. Turn the box shape to right side.*

2 *Fill the box shape with kapok and close the gap by oversewing.*

3 *Sew tiny scraps of fabric together until a large piece of fabric has been constructed.*

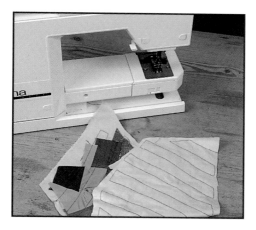

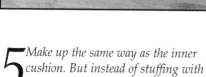

4 *Sew these tiny pieces onto a background fabric. Cut this into the same size pieces as for the inner cushion.*

5 *Make up the same way as the inner cushion. But instead of stuffing with kapok, insert the cushion.*

6 *Finish off by neatly oversewing the gap. As an alternative, before inserting the inner cushion, sew on some pockets to hold scissors, marking chalk, thimbles, tape measures etc.*

The basic waistcoat is extremely versatile and can be adapted for a festive occasion, fancy dress party or everyday wear. This one is decorated with appliqué letters and objects and is a learning tool as well as being fun to wear.

MATERIALS

Lining fabric

Felt in the following colours: Light green 84cm x 35cm (33ins x 14ins), red 10cm x 20cm (4ins x 8ins), dark green 10cm x 20cm, dark blue 10cm x 20cm, black 10cm x 20cm

A selection of threads to match the felts, sewing needle, scissors, pencil, ruler, paper for patterns, pins, pinking shears (optional)

2 Cut out the letters and motifs in the following order. From red felt, 'A' and the apple. From orange, 'C' and the carrot. From light blue, one half of the ball. From dark blue, the letter 'B' and the remaining half of the ball. From black felt cut out the apple stalk and carrot stripes.

1 Copy pattern from the back of the book onto paper and cut out. Fold the light green felt in half and pin the back of the waistcoat pattern piece along the fold line. Pin the front of the waistcoat pattern piece next to it. Cut them out.

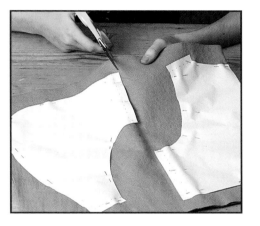

4 With right sides together, pin the front pieces to the back waistcoat piece along the side and shoulder seams and stitch 1cm from the edge. Press the seams open.

3 Pin the letters to the right-hand side of the front waistcoat and the motifs to the left-hand side. Using matching threads, stitch them into place.

T his waistcoat was ready-made. However, it is much easier to appliqué patterns onto fabric that has just been cut out and before it is finally assembled. Although it is possible to decorate an existing waistcoat, it is rather more difficult for a beginner to attempt. Before you start, buy a paper pattern for a waistcoat. The fabric in the one illustrated is a heavy raw silk.

2 Trace the template designs onto the backing paper of the fusible webbing and iron the other side onto the back of the black fabric which will make up the superimposed appliqué design.

5 Place the black shapes into position overlapping the diamond shapes where required. Remove backing iron into place and sew down. Finish off the waistcoat according to the instructions in the pattern.

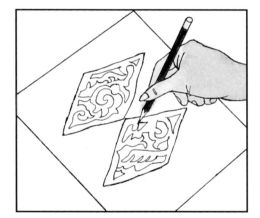

1 Copy one or both designs from the templates onto tracing paper or use a photocopier if you wish it to be larger in scale. Appliqué coloured fabrics in a striped pattern onto a backing fabric. Cut into rough diamond shapes.

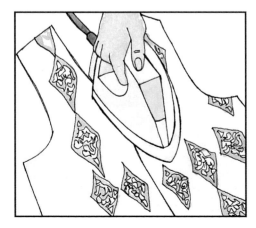

3 Using very sharp embroidery scissors, cut out the shapes to be appliquéd.

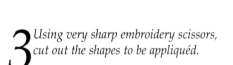

4 Peel away the backing paper and pin the coloured diamond shapes onto the waist-coat fronts. Iron the shapes into position and zig-zag stitch.

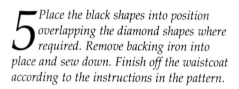

MATERIALS

Bought paper pattern for a waistcoat

Fabric according to the pattern

Dressmakers' scissors

Fabric for making appliqué

Use of a photocopier

Tracing paper

Double-sided fusible webbing

Embroidery scissors, iron, sewing-machine and thread

An inexpensive bought straw or felt hat can be given a glamorous look by adding fabric roses. Make them in luxury fabrics such as silk or satin and sew them onto the hat-band or directly onto the hat.

MATERIALS

A straw or felt hat

Pieces of fabric in complementary colours for the roses

Needle and matching thread

1 The size of the fabric you cut will depend on the size and fullness of the blooms you require. Cut strips of fabric four times as long as they are deep. With right sides together, fold the fabric in half and sew along one narrow width.

2 Turn right side out and, keeping the fabric folded neatly in half down its length and starting with the stitched end, roll the fabric three times to form the centre of the rose. Catch with a few running stitches.

3 To form the rest of the rose petals, gather the fabric at the base and catch with a few stitches, continuing until all the fabric is used. Fold in the end to neaten.

4 Make the roses in blue and purple satin and sew in alternate colours around the band of the hat.

These brightly-coloured cotton table mats will add a striking decorative feature to your table and, being machine washable, are practical too. Choose your colours to match your dining room, or the stencilled table cloth on page 30.

or the stencilled table cloth on page 30.

MATERIALS

Brightly-coloured cotton fabrics (you will need three layers for each table mat. The dimensions are your own choice)

Sewing-machine

Coloured cotton thread

Needles and pins

Scissors, tape measure, iron

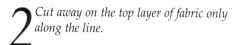

2 *Cut away on the top layer of fabric only along the line.*

1 *Cut out three layers of fabric for each table mat. The two bottom layers can be the same colour with the top layer a different contrasting shade. The top layer needs to be 1cm (½ in) bigger all round than the others. Using the template, make a paper pattern and placing it in the middle of the top layer, draw round it approximately 5-7cm (2-3ins) in from the inside edge, creating a frame effect.*

3 *Pin the three layers of fabrics together. Then turn the top, slightly larger layer, over onto the underside of the table mat. Neaten the edges. Press.*

4 *Using a sewing-machine proceed to zig-zag around the edge of the top layer on the inside decorative line. This prevents it from fraying and holds it into position. Now sew by hand or machine round the outer edge of each mat.*

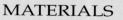

This pretty cushion is easy and fun to make and will brighten up a child's bedroom, or any room for that matter. With stencilling and added buttons, this is a good way to introduce the novice to the art of appliqué.

1 Using the template, trace the fish shape from the book. Then trace the decorative pattern onto a piece of stencil card. Cut out the pattern using a craft knife.

3 When the stencils are dry, iron on the back to fix. Cut out the fish shapes leaving a border of 0.5 cm all the way round. Cut out bubble shapes as indicated in the design and sew these and the fish onto the largest piece of calico, turning under the edges as you work. Add buttons to make the fish eyes.

2 From the large piece, cut out three pieces of calico, one 30cm x 30cm (12ins x 12ins) and two 30cm x 22cm (12ins x 9ins) to make the cushion. Cut three more pieces of coloured cotton fabric on which to stencil. Place newspaper on the work table and put the coloured fabrics on top. Place the stencil onto the fabric and, holding the stencil brush vertically, stamp through the stencil onto the fabric below. Lift the stencil paper off the design, being careful not to smudge it, and leave to dry.

4 Make the cushion cover by neatening one edge of each of the two smaller pieces of calico. Place these two small pieces so that their neat edges overlap. With right sides together, place the two pieces with the overlap in the centre onto the larger piece with all the edges matching. This creates an envelope back. Sew all round the edge and then turn right side out.

MATERIALS

An inexpensive photograph album or notebook (Ours measures 35cm x 30cm (13¾ ins x 11¾ ins), but sizes could be adjusted according to your requirements

50cm x 90cm (20ins x 36ins) fabric for the cover

Iron-on double-sided fusible webbing

45cm x 10cm (18ins x 4ins) wide ribbon and 45cm x 2.5cm (18ins x 1in) ribbon in a contrast colour for centre of spine.

Scraps of different coloured fabrics for appliqué

Beads, shells and/or star fish

Fabric glue, thread and needles

Dressmakers' tracing paper, vilene

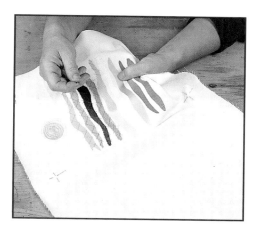

Endless care goes into taking holiday photographs, recording family events, or even collecting recipes only to later find they have been mislaid. Why not make this personalized album and keep you treasures safe and always to hand.

3 Decorate over the wave shapes with large Xs.

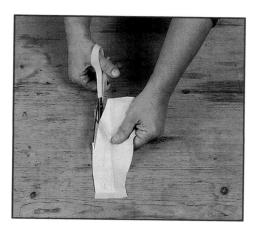

1 Iron the double-sided fusible webbing onto the fabric scraps and draw the design onto the paper backing. With sharp embroidery scissors, cut out the shapes.

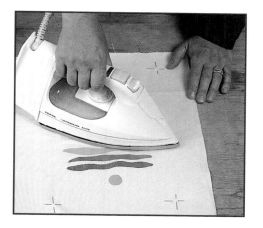

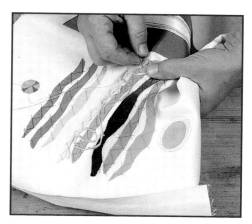

4 Add embroidery and other objects such as wool, shells etc.

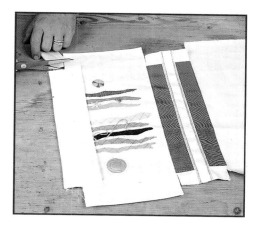

2 Iron a piece of calico fabric measuring 88cm x 39.7cm (35½ ins x 15¾ ins) onto a piece of (vilene) interfacing. Tack a vertical line down the centre. Then tack a parallel line 5cm (2ins) to the right. This line marks the front edge of the cover. Using pins as shown, mark out the other three edges of the front cover. This produces a frame in which to add your appliquéd elements. Taking your shapes, remove the paper backing, place on the front cover and iron into place.

5 To finish the album cover: Cut a 31cm (13ins) length of 10cm (4ins) wide ribbon and tack it so that it covers the vertical left-hand row of tacking stitches, stopping slightly short of the top and bottom of the album. Sew into place with a close set zig-zag stitch. 1cm from the sides of the ribbon spine cut down 4.5cm or as near to the top and bottom of the zig-zag stitching as you can go. To make the album flaps: Fold in the right and left edges by 8cm (3ins) so that the right sides of the fabric are together, pin and then machine across the fold 4cm below the top edge and above the bottom edge. Trim the folded 8cm to within 6mm of the stitching. Turn outside in to form the sleeves and push the cover into its jacket. To finish, glue the centre flaps to the inside of the spine and glue the other edges to the inside of the front and back covers.

MATERIALS

1m (39ins) plasticized fabric

*1.60m (64ins) cotton tape
cut in eight pieces*

*Wide bias binding, sufficient to
edge the mat*

3.75m (150ins) piping cord

*Pieces of plasticized sticky-backed
material in a variety of colours*

1 *Take the plasticized fabric. Fold it into quarters and draw a quarter circle using a piece of string and a pencil. Cut through all four thicknesses. Open out, and you have a circle. Sew the bias binding all round the edges. Mark at even intervals round the circle and sew the loops to the wrong side of the mat.*

2 *Trace the design on to the backing paper of the sticky backed plastic and cut out.*

This PVC mat is ideal for picnics. It has loops round its edge threaded with a drawstring so that it can also be used as a storage bag.

3 *Turn under the edge of the bias and sew all round the mat to neaten the edge. Cut out the shapes as shown in the photograph. Stick them down on the mat.*

4 *Thread the cord through the loops and tie the ends together.*

MATERIALS

A marbling bath – a photographic developing tray is good for this purpose

Tap water, marbling kit consisting of thickener and marbling colours

White fabric (fine silk or satin is best) or a ready-made bow tie

Clothes line and pegs, iron, knitting needle for stirring the colours

Marbling can be done using a kit which includes a thickener and marbling colours. The best fabrics on which to marble are silk and satin. Alternatively, you can apply this treatment to a ready-made, plain, light-coloured bow tie.

1 *Mix two heaped teaspoons of the thickening powder with one litre of water and leave to stand for at least one hour. Pour the resulting mixture into the marbling frame or bath until the depth of the mixture is 1½ to 2ins deep.*

2 *Wash the fabric or the bow tie to get rid of any size or dressing. Hang it up to dry. When the fabric is dry, iron it with a cool iron.*

3 *Using an eye dropper or pipette, drop the chosen colours onto the surface of the gel. The colours will float on the surface and spread slowly out from the centre. If you drop too much colour it will sink to the bottom.*

4 *When the surface is full of colour, make patterns by swirling or combing the paint with a knitting needle. It is a good idea to keep a record of which colours look good together and the way in which you treated them.*

5 *Lay the fabric on top of the medium so that the centre of the cloth touches it first. Let the edges fall into place. Do not move the fabric or the pattern will be disturbed. Most fabric looks translucent when wet so you should be able to see any areas where the pattern has not taken. Very gently touch the back of the cloth so that it makes contact with the medium. Lift the cloth off vertically so that the pattern is not disturbed. Leave to dry.*

6 *Rinse under a tap and leave to dry once more. When the fabric is dry, iron it on the back to fix.*

MATERIALS
40cm (16ins) square of fabric,
2 pieces of fabric 40cm x 30cm (16ins x 12ins)

Scraps of fabrics in contrast colours

Needle, thread, pins, sewing-machine

T his unusual cushion is decorated with plaits of fabric which have been coiled and used as a form of decoration.

1 Cut lengths of fabrics approx 1cm wide. Pin them together in threes and plait turning in the edges as you do. Make nine plaits in all and pin them to the cushion front in coils.

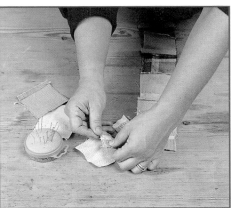

2 Sew them onto the cushion down the centre of each coil to prevent them from coming undone.

3 Cut small oblong scraps and sew these together to make a border.

4 Pin these onto the cushion so that they surround the plaits.

5 Turn under all the edges and sew the border onto the cushion using a zig-zag stitch. Make up the cushion back by neatening one 40cm (16in) edge of each of the remaining fabric pieces. These make the back opening. Overlap them and sew the other edges so they match up with the cushion front.

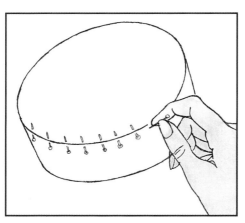

1 To make the crown pattern, draw a 20.3cm (8ins) diameter circle onto paper and cut out. Measure and cut a paper hat-band 70cm x 8cm (27¹⁄₂ins x 3ins). Pin the crown to the hat-band, try it on, and adjust to fit. Pin the pattern pieces onto the lining, wadding, and top fabric and cut out one circle and one band from each.

These elegant smoking caps are popular with both men and women. Once you have worked out the basic technique you can use this example to create your own designs.

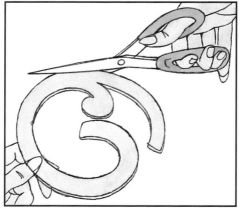

2 Trace the template design onto the backing paper of the fusible webbing. Iron onto the contrast fabric following the manufacturer's instructions for temperature. Cut out the design.

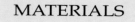
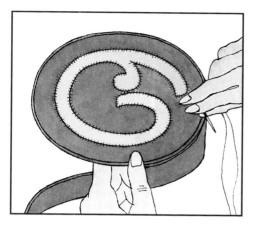

7 *With the right sides together, pin and then baste the hat-band to the crown. Try on and adjust if necessary. Sew the two ends of the band together and then sew the crown to the band.*

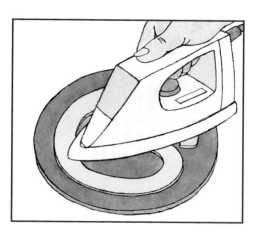

3 *Pull off the backing paper and iron the motif onto the crown and the hat-band.*

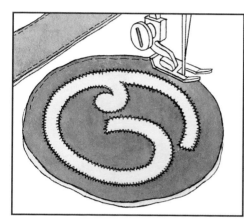

5 *Sew the appliquéd fabric to the wadding with the appliqué on top and the wadding underneath. Sew round the edge of the hat-band and the crown.*

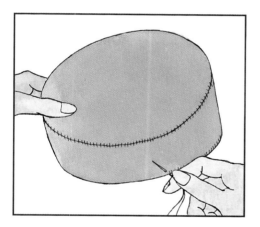

8 *With the cap inside out, sew the lining band to the crown and then fit in the hat. Neaten by oversewing along the bottom edge.*

4 *Set the machine to a close zig-zag and appliqué the motifs into place.*

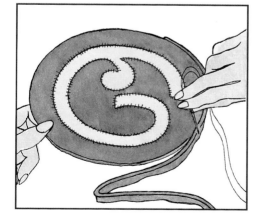

6 *Cut the piping cord in half and cover with bias cut fabric, then sew it around the edge of the crown.*

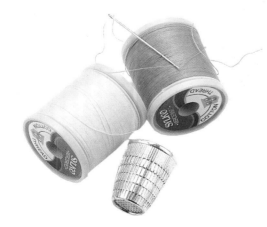

Personalize your silk lingerie. Silk painting is not only very easy but gives a professional result and can brighten-up an otherwise lacklustre garment.

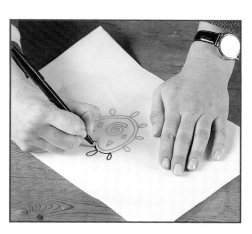

1 Make up a design of your own choice and place onto tracing paper using a very dark felt tip pen.

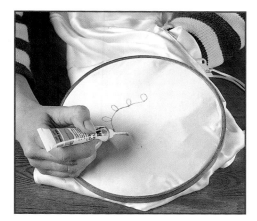

2 Stretch the piece of lingerie, where you wish to decorate it, over the embroidery hoop. Tape the design to the underside of the lingerie – you should be able to see the motif through the silk. Trace over the design with the gutta outliner. Leave to dry.

3 Remove the paper and fill in the space between the gutta outliner with the silk paints. This will prevent the silk paints from spreading beyond its barrier.

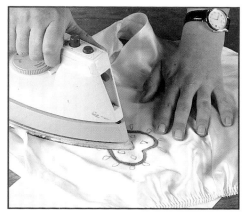

4 Leave to dry, then remove the lingerie from the hoop and iron on the back to fix, or follow the manufacturer's instructions for their silk paints.

Make your children these richly-decorated Christmas stockings which will add a festive appeal to your fireplace. Use any scraps of material and trimmings you may have to hand. They are simplicity itself to make and have a really expensive look about them.

3 Cut out brightly-coloured fabric of your choice and pin into place. Do not overlap the fabric too much.

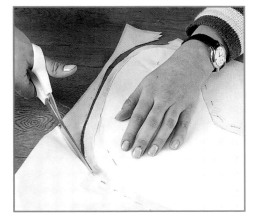

1 Enlarge up the stocking template in the back of the book to the size you require and trace onto pattern paper.

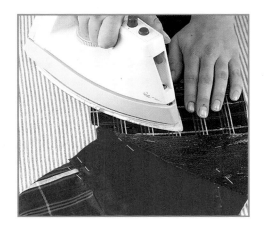

4 Following the manufacturer's instructions, iron the fabric onto the interfacing.

6 Turn the two halves back to back and sew together leaving 1cm seam allowance. Hem the top. Turn the right way round and finish off the top with coloured cord and a loop to hang on the fireplace.

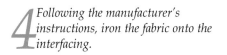

2 Place the iron-on interfacing back to back, pin the pattern on and cut out.

5 Cover the rough edges with ric-rac, coloured ribbon and binding. Pin in place and then sew on.

7 As a finishing touch, sew on coloured beads and baubles to give an extra festive feel.

APPLIQUÉ CUSHIONS

These exquisite cushions are decorated with bonded appliqué. The technique will enable you to work intricate and complicated designs with the minimum of effort.

Make a cushion in velvet for a luxurious sitting room sofa or in cottons or natural fabrics for use in the dining room or kitchen. The designs can be as sophisticated as you like, or simple and jolly in bright colours for a child's room or nursery.

MATERIALS

Cushion pad, enough velvet to cover the back and front of the cushion, pieces of contrast fabric, gold edging

Double-sided fusible webbing, pins, tailor's chalk, sewing thread, sewing-machine, dressmaking and embroidery scissors

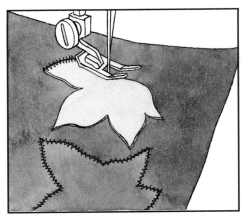

3 Set the machine to a close zig-zag stitch along the edge of each motif covering the raw edges as you sew. Finish off the design by sewing on gold edging.

1 Cut the cushion front and back so they are 1cm larger all round than the cushion pad dimensions. Iron the interfacing onto the back of the contrast fabrics and trace the leaf and squiggle designs onto the backing paper.

2 Cut the shapes and peel the backing paper off and place them on the front of the cushion cover so that they make an attractive design. Iron them into place to secure them.

4 Make up the cushion. With the right sides facing, sew the front to the back of the cushion around three sides. Turn the right way round and insert the cushion pad and sew up the opening using an oversew stitch.

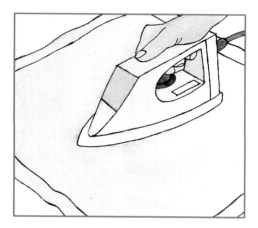

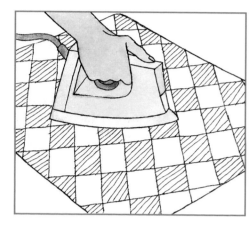

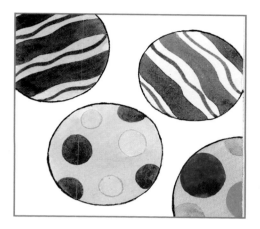

1 Cut the cushion front and back so that they are 1cm larger all round than the cushion pad dimensions. Using the extra 50cm of the same fabric, iron on the interfacing.

3 Cut the wavy lines into diamond shapes. Pick the paper off and place the diamonds on the front of the cushion cover. Iron the diamonds into place to secure them. Using a close zig-zag stitch, sew round the edges of the diamonds.

4 To cover the buttons, appliqué fabrics in contrasting colours and cut large enough to fit over the buttons. Fit the buttons according to the manufacturer's instructions. (Continue overleaf)

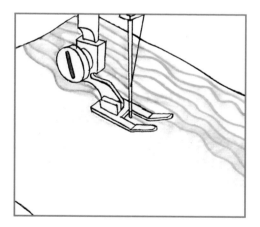

2 Place the interfaced fabric under the sewing-machine, and in a contrast colour sew wavy lines up and down the fabric.

MATERIALS

Cushion pad, cotton or linen in a natural-coloured fabric sufficient to cover the back and front of the cushion, plus another 50cm (20ins), or so, of small pieces of contrast fabrics, buttons for covering, coloured bias binding

Double-sided fusible webbing, pins, tailors, chalk, sewing thread, sewing machine, dressmaking and embroidery scissors

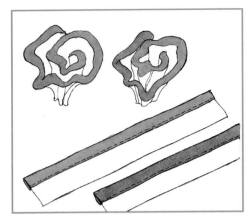

5 *Make other buttons by edging 7cm (2³⁄₄ in) x 1.5cm (¹⁄₂ in) strips with bias binding and gathering these into spirals.*

6 *Sew the spirals and the buttons and appliqué shapes of your choice at the points of the diamonds.*

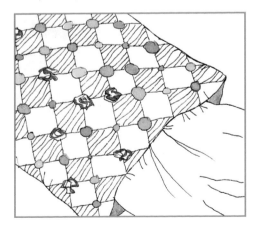

7 *Make up the cushion. With the right sides facing, sew the front to the back of the cushion around three sides. Turn to the right side, insert the cushion pad and sew up the opening using an overstitch.*

H ave fun making and wearing this fun belt. An ideal use for all your old buttons.

MATERIALS

100cm x 6.25cm (40ins x 2½ins) black-and-white striped fabric

White cotton webbing

20-40 buttons of different kinds

Needle, sewing thread, pencil, ruler, scissors

Cover buckle kit

3 eyelets and tool to insert them

1 On the back of the striped fabric, measure a rectangle 90cm x 6.25cm (35 ½ins x 2 ½ins). Cut it out. With right sides facing, fold the fabric in half so that the longest edges meet. Press along the fold line. Cut one end of the webbing to a point. Lay the point ¼in away from one end of the folded belt fabric with one long edge of the webbing against the fold line. Pin the webbing to the belt fabric. Mark the point onto the fabric with a pencil.

4 Arrange the buttons along the right side of the belt and with extra strong thread stitch them into place.

3 Insert 3 eyelets starting 2ins from the point and spacing them 2ins apart. Cover the belt buckle, following the instructions on the packet. Attach the buckle to the belt: Measure 1¼ins from the straight end of the belt and snip a ½in slit in the centre of the belt. Buttonhole-stitch the slit and insert the prong of the belt buckle.

2 Remove the pins and the webbing. Keep the fabric folded and stitch along this line. Turn the belt fabric the right way out and use scissors to push out the pointed end. Insert the point of the webbing into the point of the belt. Pin the webbing into the fabric belt to stop it moving. Turn in the top ¼in raw edge and tack down. Edge stitch around the belt.

ELEPHANT CUSHION page 22

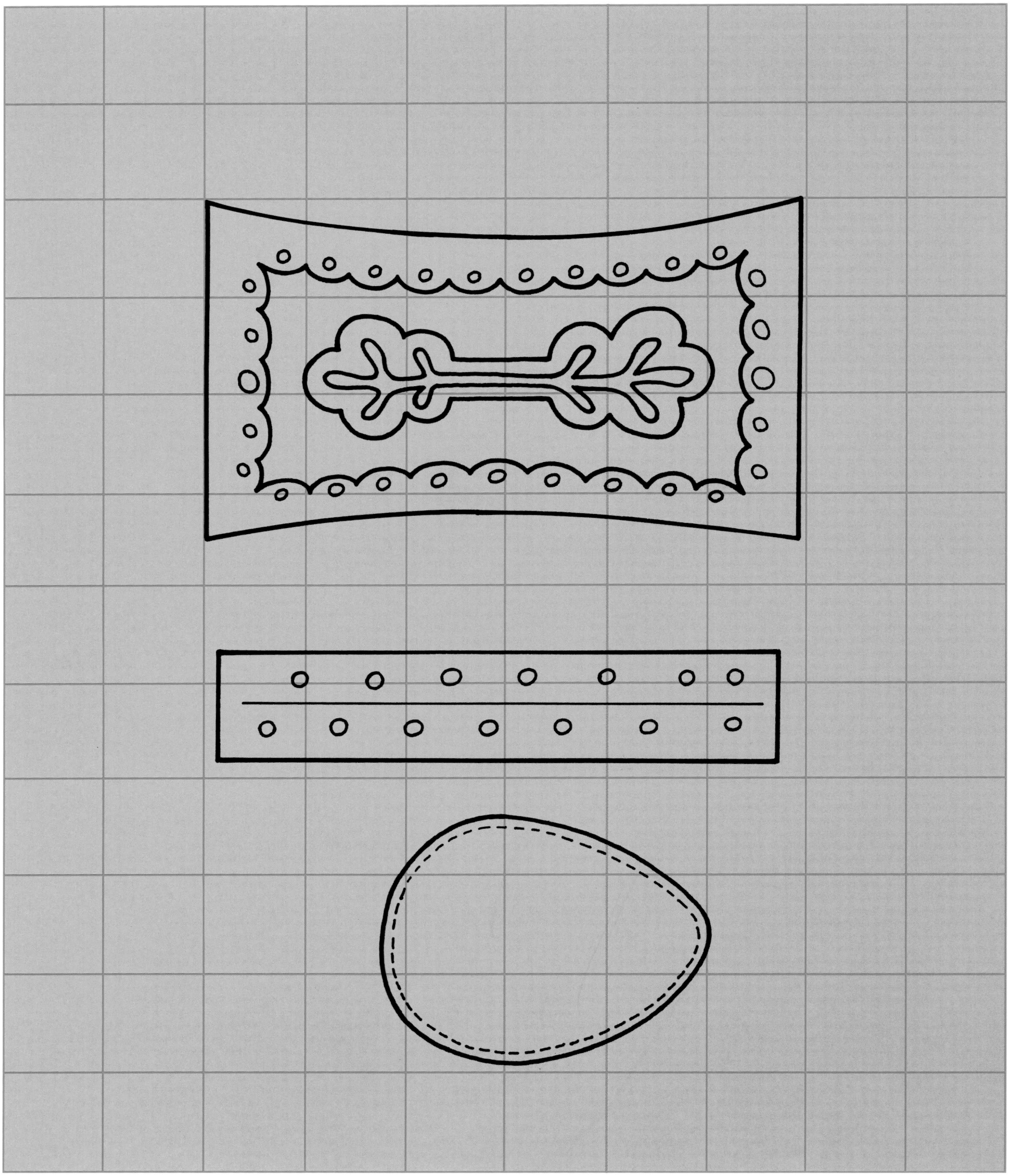

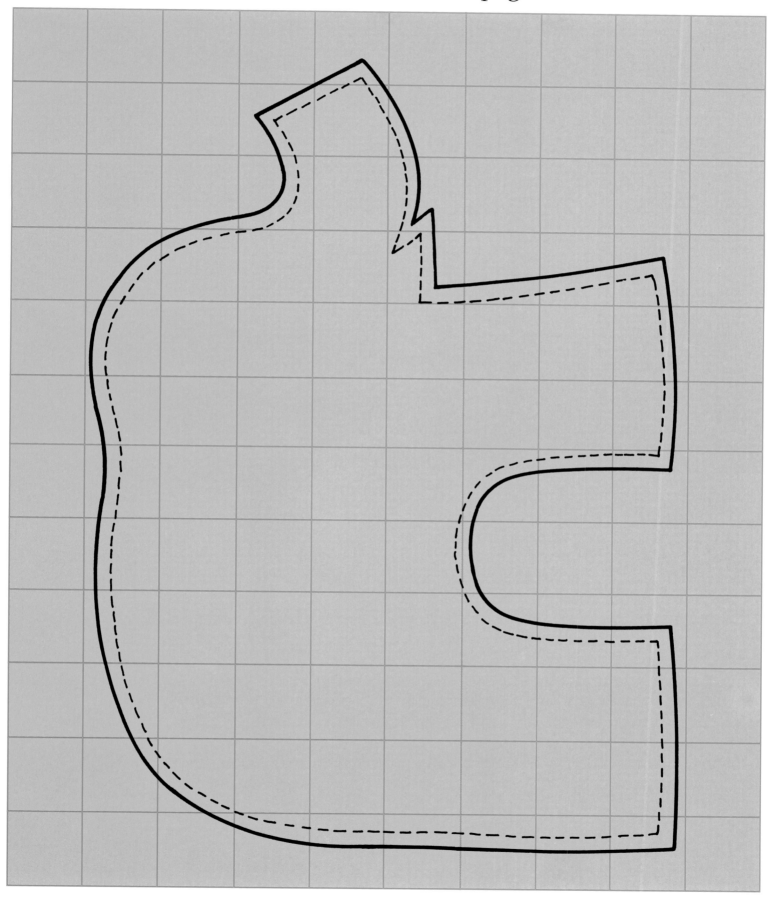

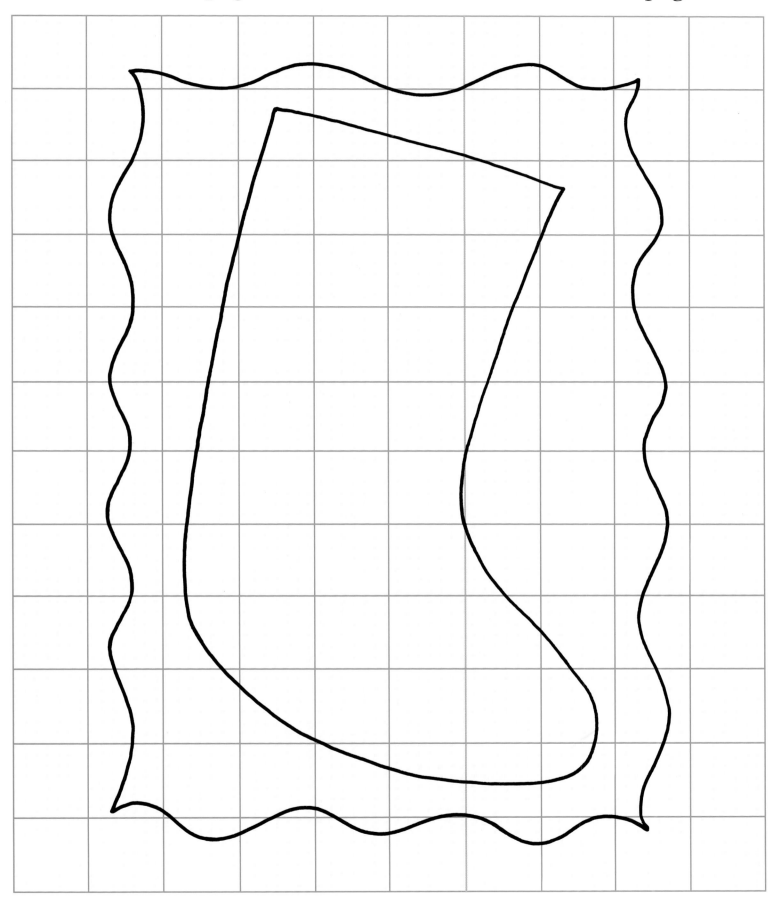

CHILD'S APRON page 16

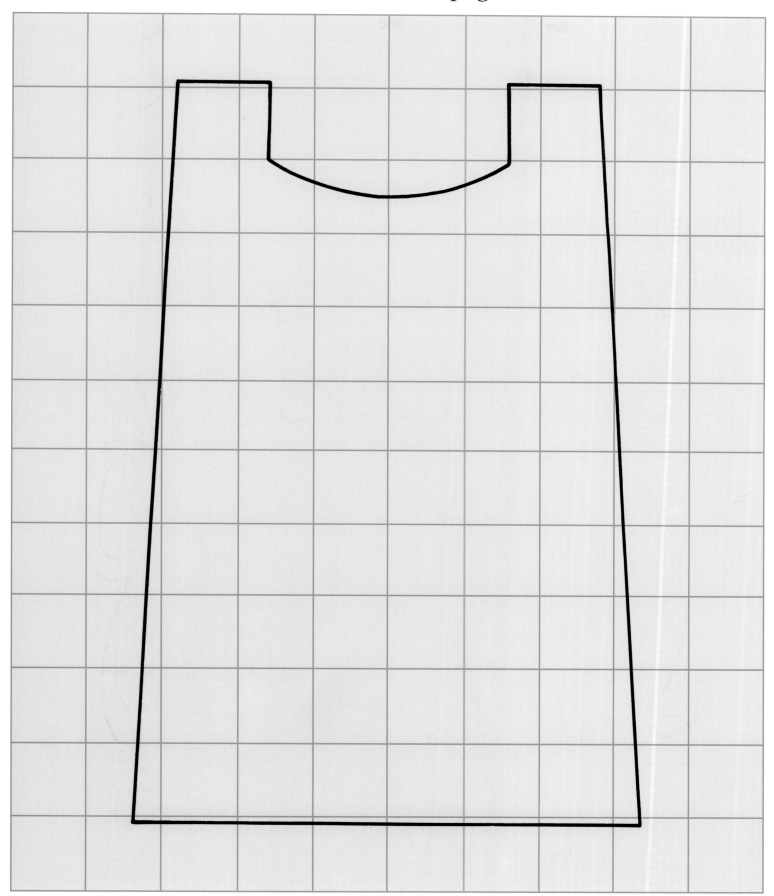

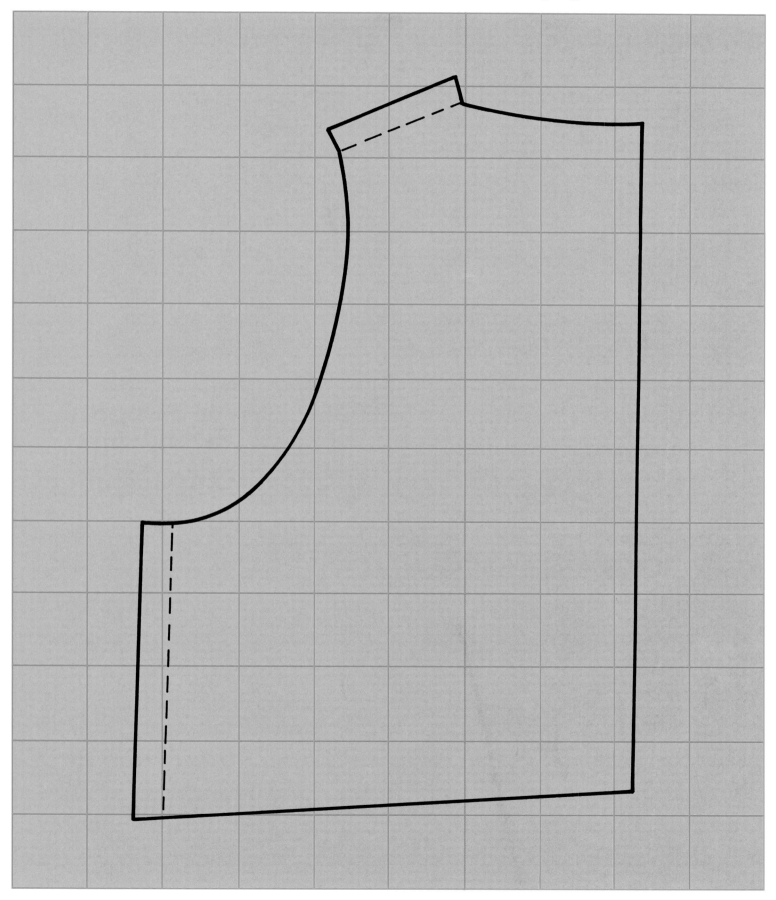